ARTIFICIAL INTELLIGENCE: RECENT TRENDS AND TECHNIQUES

DR S MEERA

Contents

CHAPTER ONE

Introduction to Artificial Intelligence

What is Artificial Intelligence?

Artificial intelligence (AI) is the ability of a computer program or a machine to think and learn. It has been defined in many ways, but in general it can be described as a way of making a computer system "smart" – that is, able to understand complex tasks and carry out complex commands.

Artificial intelligence is a branch of computer science that deals with the creation of intelligent machines that work and react like humans.

Artificial intelligence (AI) is the ability of a computer program or a machine to think and learn. It is a branch of computer science that deals with the creation of intelligent machines that work and react like humans.

Philosophy of AI

The philosophy of AI is the study of the nature of intelligence, its properties and its implications for understanding the mind and artificial intelligence. It raises questions about the nature of intelligence, its relationship to the mind and to artificial intelligence, and about the proper methodology for its study.

The philosophy of AI is closely related to the philosophy of mind, and to the more general field of philosophy of cognition. AI researchers and philosophers of mind have long been engaged in a lively debate about the relationship between mind and intelligence. The central question in this debate is whether intelligence is best understood as a property of the mind or as a property of the brain.

The mind-brain debate is relevant to the philosophy of AI in two ways. First, if intelligence is a property of the mind, then AI research is concerned with understanding the nature of the mind. Second, if intelligence is a property of the brain, then AI research is concerned with understanding the brain and its workings.

The philosophy of AI is also closely related to the field of cognitive science. Cognitive science is the study of the mind and its mental processes, including intelligence. The cognitive sciences include disciplines such as psychology, neuroscience, and artificial intelligence.

The philosophy of AI is also related to the field of philosophy of science. The philosophy of science is concerned with the nature of scientific knowledge and its methods of acquisition. The philosophy of AI is concerned with the nature of AI knowledge and its methods of acquisition.

The philosophy of AI is also related to the field of philosophy of technology. The philosophy of technology is concerned with the nature of technology and its implications for society. The philosophy of AI is concerned with the nature of AI technology and its implications for society.

Goals of AI:

The goals of AI are to create intelligent agents, which are systems that reason, learn, and act autonomously.

Some of the specific goals of AI include:

1. Developing agents that can reason and learn autonomously

2. Developing agents that can interact with humans naturally

3. Developing agents that can autonomously solve problems

4. Developing agents that can reason probabilistically

5. Developing agents that can learn from experience

What Contributes to AI?

There are many things that contribute to artificial intelligence. One of the most important is the ability to process and store data. AI systems need large amounts of data in order to learn and improve their performance. Another important factor is the ability to perform complex computations.

AI systems need to be able to perform calculations that are too difficult for humans to do. Finally, AI systems need to be able to interact with the world. They need to be able to perceive their environment and take actions that achieve their goals.

There are a number of factors that contribute to artificial intelligence, including but not limited to: data, algorithms, computing power, and human expertise

There is no single answer to this question as there are many factors that can contribute to the development of artificial intelligence. Some of the most important factors include the availability of data, the development of algorithms, and the computing power required to run these algorithms.

Programming Without and With AI :

Artificial intelligence is a field of computer science and engineering focused on the creation of intelligent agents, which are systems that can reason, learn, and act autonomously.

AI research deals with the question of how to create computers that are capable of intelligent behaviour. In practical terms, AI applications can be deployed in a number of ways, including:

1. **Machine learning:** This is a method of teaching computers to learn from data, without being explicitly programmed.

2. **Natural language processing:** This involves teaching computers to understand human language and respond in a way that is natural for humans.

3. **Robotics:** This involves the use of robots to carry out tasks that would otherwise be difficult or impossible for humans to do.

4. **Predictive analytics:** This is a method of using artificial intelligence to make predictions about future events, trends, and behaviors.

5. **Computer vision:** This is the ability of computers to interpret and understand digital images.

What is AI Technique?

The ATA has been working on this for years, but it has been a slow process because of the lack of resources. The ATA does have a working definition for AI:

"Artificial Intelligence is the ability of a machine to accurately analyze and process data, as well as make decisions based on that data."

The ATA has also been working on developing a process to include this definition into the ATA Certification Program, so that translators can be certified as AI experts.

What Can Translators Do to Prepare for AI?

The best thing that translators can do is to stay informed. Read about new developments in AI, and learn about the different applications that are currently being used. There are many articles and blog posts about AI, so there is no shortage of information out there.

The other thing that translators can do is to learn about the different tools that are available. There are many different software programs that are designed to help translators with their work. Some of these programs are designed to help with translation memory, while others are designed to help with terminology management.

The bottom line is that translators need to be prepared for the future. AI is going to have a major impact on the translation industry, and it is important for translators to be prepared for the changes that are coming.

Applications of AI :

Artificial intelligence is used in a variety of applications, including:

Speech recognition

Speech recognition is the interdisciplinary subfield of computational linguistics that develops methodologies and technologies that enables the recognition and translation of spoken language into text by computers.

Fraud detection

Fraud detection or prevention is a major use case for data science. Financial institutions, e-commerce platforms, and social media sites all need to be able to identify fraudulent behavior. Data science can help these organizations identify patterns in data that may indicate fraudulent behavior.

Predictive maintenance

Predictive maintenance is defined as a maintenance strategy that uses condition monitoring and diagnostics to predict the remaining useful life of critical components and systems. The goal of predictive maintenance is to avoid the costly and unplanned downtime associated with reactive maintenance.

Autonomous vehicles

Autonomous vehicles will have to be able to drive smoothly, safely and efficiently in a wide range of conditions, including dense traffic, poor weather, construction sites, and etc. To achieve this, researchers are working on a range of technologies, including GPS, radar, sonar, Lidar, and computer vision.

History of AI:

The history of artificial intelligence (AI) begins in antiquity, with myths, stories and rumors of artificial beings endowed with intelligence or consciousness by master craftsmen. The modern history of AI begins more concretely in the 1950s, with a number of workshops, conferences, and publications.

The field of AI research was founded at a Dartmouth College conference in 1956. Since then, AI has had several waves of popularity, followed by periods of relative neglect.

The first wave of AI research was sparked by the Dartmouth conference and lasted until the early 1970s. This period saw significant progress in the development of AI programs, including the creation of the first expert systems, the first logic-based AI programming language, and the first AI machine learning programs.

The second wave of AI began in the late 1970s and lasted through the 1980s. This was a period of intense research into AI applications, including expert systems, natural language processing and machine learning.

The third wave of AI, which began in the early 1990s, was characterized by a focus on artificial neural networks and biologically inspired models. This wave also saw the first commercial applications of AI, such as expert systems for business and medicine.

The fourth wave of AI, which is currently used by us.

CHAPTER TWO

Roles of Intelligent Agents

What is Intelligence?

The definition of intelligence is difficult to define, because intelligence has multiple definitions. Some say that intelligence is the power of learning. Others define intelligence as the ability to think abstractly.

The definition of intelligence is difficult to define, because intelligence has multiple definitions. Some say that intelligence is the power of learning. Others define intelligence as the ability to think abstractly.

Types of Intelligence

There are three different types of intelligence:

Fluid intelligence

Fluid intelligence is the ability to reason and solve problems independently of prior knowledge or experience. This type of intelligence is often used in problem-solving tasks that require creative thinking, such as puzzles or brainteasers.

Crystallized intelligence

Crystallized intelligence is the ability to learn from experience and apply that knowledge to new situations. It is the ability to see the world in new ways and to find new solutions to problems. It is the ability to think abstractly and to see relationships between things.

Emotional intelligence

Emotional intelligence (EI) has been defined as "the capacity to be aware of and manage one's own emotions, and the emotions of others" (Mayer & Salovey, 1997).EI is a relatively new concept that is still being researched and developed. However, there is evidence to suggest that EI can be a powerful predictor of success in life.

For example, a study of over 1,000 people found that those with higher levels of EI were more likely to be successful in their careers and relationships (Cherniss, 2010).

EI has also been linked to better health, as those with higher EI are more likely to take care of their physical and mental health (Mayer & Salovey, 1997).

What is Intelligence composed of?

The definition of intelligence is difficult to define, because intelligence has multiple definitions. Some say that intelligence is the power of learning. Others define intelligence as the ability to think abstractly

Difference between Human and Machine Intelligence.

The main difference between human and machine intelligence is that human intelligence is based on the ability to learn from experience and remember information, while machine intelligence is based on the ability to process large amounts of data and recognize patterns.

Human intelligence is the ability of a human being to think, reason, and perceive. Machine intelligence is the ability of a machine to perform tasks that would normally require human intelligence, such as reasoning, natural language processing, and problem solving.

CHAPTER THREE

Research Areas of Artificial Intelligence

Speech Recognition:

Speech recognition involves the automatic conversion of spoken language into written text. It can be used as part of a human-machine interface, in which a user speaks commands to a computer or other device and the device responds accordingly.

Speech recognition can also be used in biometrics, in which an individual's voice is used as a unique identifier to confirm their identity.

Speech recognition systems are typically based on Hidden Markov Models (HMMs). HMMs are statistical models that describe the behavior of a sequence of observations, such as a series of speech sounds. The models are used to estimate the likelihood of a sequence of observations, such as a particular utterance, and can be trained using a set of known samples.

Voice Recognition:

Voice recognition is similar to speech recognition, but is typically used to identify an individual based on their voice rather than to transcribe speech.

Voice recognition systems are often used in security applications, such as to unlock a door or to access a computer. Voice recognition systems are typically based on Gaussian Mixture Models (GMMs).

Working of Speech and Voice Recognition Systems:

Speech and voice recognition systems work on the basis of a set of mathematical algorithms known as acoustic models. These algorithms take into account various aspects of the sound waveform, such as pitch, spectral shape, and energy distribution, and then analyze it to generate a set of feature vectors, which are then used to identify the speech.

The feature vectors generated by the acoustic models are then compared with a set of reference vectors, which are stored in a database. If there is a match between the two sets of vectors, then the speech is recognized.

Real Life Applications of Research Areas:

The research areas in this report have a variety of real-world applications. In general, the applications fall into one of three categories:

1) Improving understanding of how humans interact with technology

2) Developing new technologies or improving existing technologies

3) Improving the effectiveness of human-technology systems

Improving Understanding of How Humans Interact with Technology

Many of the research areas in this report can be used to improve understanding of how humans interact with technology. This understanding can be used to improve the design of technologies, to develop training programs for users of technologies, and to develop policies for the use of technologies.

For example, research on human factors in aviation can be used to improve the design of aircraft and air traffic control systems. This research can also be used to develop training programs for pilots and air traffic controllers.

Similarly, research on human factors in healthcare can be used to improve the design of medical devices and healthcare information systems. This research can also be used to develop training programs for healthcare providers.

Task Classification of AI

There are many different types of AI tasks, but they can generally be classified into three broad categories:

Perceptual tasks

Perceptual tasks are tasks that require an individual to use their sense to identify or discriminate between different stimuli.

Examples of perceptual tasks include:

* Visual tasks, such as identifying different colours or shapes

* Auditory tasks, such as discriminating between different sounds

* Tactile tasks, such as identifying different textures

* Olfactory tasks, such as identifying different smells

Cognitive tasks

Cognitive task analysis (CTA) is a structured process that can be used to generate a detailed description of how experts solve a problem or perform a task. It is often used to develop training materials or to assess the usability of a system.

The goal of CTA is to identify the critical steps and decisions that experts use to complete a task, as well as the knowledge and skills required. This information can then be used to design training programs or to improve the design of systems.

CTA generally consists of four steps:

1. Task analysis: The first step is to identify the task or problem to be analyzed. This may involve observing experts as they perform the task, interviewing them about the task, or reviewing documents or manuals.

2. Cognitive analysis: The second step is to understand the mental processes that experts use to complete the task. This may involve interviews, think-aloud protocols, or other methods.

3. Representation: The third step is to represent the information from the cognitive analysis in a form that can be used to design training programs or improve system design.

4. Evaluation: The fourth step is to evaluate the effectiveness of the training program or system design. This may involve observing users as they complete the task

Motor tasks

The movement tasks of the arm, the leg, the trunk and the head are combined in the brain. This task is called motor task.

CHAPTER FOUR

Agents and Environments

What are Agent and Environment?

Agent and Environment are the two fundamental elements of Reinforcement Learning. The agent is the entity that interacts with the environment. The environment is everything that the agent can affect.

In artificial intelligence, an agent is a piece of software that is designed to autonomously perform tasks or achieve goals. The agent can be either a stand-alone program or a component of a larger system.

The environment is the agent's surrounding context, including both physical and virtual elements. The environment provides the agent with information about its surroundings and the ability to interact with those surroundings.

Agents Terminology

The term agent is used in a variety of ways throughout this document.

Agent: An instance of the Oracle Endeca MDEX Engine that provides indexing, search, and navigation capabilities.

Content Provider Agent: An agent that provides content to a Content Analytics Agent, Data Discovery Agent, or

Data Transformation Agent for indexing, search, and navigation. Content provider agents can be either local or remote to the agent they are providing content to.

Content Analytics Agent: An agent that uses the Content Analytics Module to perform content analytics operations.

Data Discovery Agent: An agent that uses the Data Discovery Module to perform data discovery operations.

Data Transformation Agent: An agent that uses the Data Transformation Module to perform data transformation operations.

Rationality:

Rationality is a complex concept which has been the subject of considerable debate. It can be defined in a number of ways. A simple definition of rationality is the capacity to act in a way that produces the best possible results, according to some person's preferences.

This definition is too simplistic, however, because people's preferences may not be consistent with one another or with some objective standards, and because people may not be able to predict the consequences of their actions.

What is Ideal Rational Agent?

In game theory and economic theory, an ideal rational agent is a theoretical construct used to model strategic decision-making. An ideal rational agent is one who always makes the best possible decision given the available information.

The Structure of Intelligent Agents

The structure of intelligent agents is designed to provide services to a variety of users. Intelligent agents are designed to perform a range of tasks, including monitoring, managing, and coordinating resources. Intelligent agents are also designed to provide information to users and to interact with other agents

. Intelligent agents are composed of a number of components, including a user interface, a knowledge base, a reasoning engine, and a set of heuristics. The user interface is responsible for providing a way for users to interact with the agent. The knowledge base is responsible for storing information about the agent's environment.

The reasoning engine is responsible for making decisions based on the information in the knowledge base. The set of heuristics is responsible for guiding the agent's search for solutions to problems.

Intelligent agents are designed to be modular, so that they can be easily extended to support new tasks and new user interfaces. Intelligent agents are also designed to be portable, so that they can be run on a variety of platforms.

Simple Reflex Agents

The agent has full observability

The agent's actions are single, discrete, and instantaneous

The agent has perfect memory

The agent is rational and will attempt to maximize its current reward

A simple reflex agent will take the action that results in the highest reward, given the current state that it is in.

Model-Based Reflex Agents

A model-based reflex agent is an agent that bases its decisions on a model of the environment.

The agent tracks the Agent tracks the expected reward for each state and makes the decision that will lead to the highest expected reward.

Goal-Based Agents:

Goal-based agents are those agents that are designed to achieve a specific goal. A goal-based agent will have a set of goals that it is trying to achieve and will use a variety of methods to achieve these goals.

Proactive Agents:

Proactive agents are those agents that take action in order to achieve their goals. Proactive agents are different from goal-based agents in that they do not just rely on their goals to guide their actions, but they also take initiative to achieve their goals.

Reactive Agents:

Reactive agents are those agents that do not take initiative to achieve their goals, but instead they react to the environment around them.

Reactive agents are different from proactive agents in that they do not take action in order to achieve their goals, but instead they wait for the environment to change in order to achieve their goals.

Utility-Based Agents

A utility-based agent is an agent that always tries to maximize some notion of utility. A utility function is a function that assigns a real number to each state, indicating the degree of desirability of that state. A utility-based agent always tries to maximize the expected utility of the outcomes it can obtain by its actions.

In utility-based agents, there are two types of decision making methods:

1. Value iteration
2. Policy iteration

Value iteration is a method used for computing the optimal policy for a given MDP, given its full definition. Policy iteration consists of two steps: policy evaluation and policy improvement.

The Nature of Environments

The physical environment refers to the natural world and the built environment refers to the human-made world. The natural environment includes all living and non-living things that occur naturally on Earth. The built environment is everything that has been constructed by humans. It includes buildings, roads, and other man-made structures.

The physical environment can be further divided into two categories: the biophysical environment and the abiotic environment. The biophysical environment includes all living things, such as plants and animals. The abiotic environment includes all non-living things, such as water, air, and soil.

The biophysical environment is essential for the survival of all living things. Plants produce oxygen and food, while animals provide food and other resources. The abiotic environment is also necessary for life, as it provides the resources that plants and animals need to survive.

The physical environment is constantly changing. The climate is affected by the Earth's position in space, as well as the amount of sunlight and greenhouse gases in the atmosphere. The changes in the physical environment can impact the biophysical environment, which in turn can affect the abiotic environment.

The human impact on the environment is also constantly changing. As the population grows and technology advances,

Turing Test :

The Turing Test is a test for artificial intelligence in which a human judge engages in a natural language conversation with one human and one machine, each of which is trying to appear human. If the judge cannot reliably tell which is which, then the machine is said to have passed the test.

Properties of Environment:

The environment consists of all the external factors that affect the organism.

The environment can be divided into two types:

1. The abiotic environment: It includes all the non-living factors such as light, temperature, water, soil, etc.

2. The biotic environment: It includes all the living factors such as plants, animals, etc.

CHAPTER FIVE

Algorithms in Artificial Intelligence

Single Agent Path finding Problems:

Single agent path finding problems are problems in which we are concerned with finding a path for a single agent from a start state to a goal state.

The agent is not concerned with others around it, and so the path it takes may or may not be optimal with respect to the other agents.

Brute-Force Search Strategies:

Many problems in computer science can be viewed as a search for a solution through a large space of possible solutions. Some of the simplest searching algorithms are those that use brute force; they try every possible option until they find a solution. Brute-force search algorithms are guaranteed to find a solution if one exists, but they may require a very long time to do so.

Breadth-First Search:

The breadth-first search algorithm is one of the simplest algorithms for searching a graph. It starts at the root node and explores all of the neighbor nodes at the present depth before moving on to the nodes at the next depth level.

Depth-First Search:

The depth-first search algorithm is another algorithm for searching a graph. It starts at the root node and explores as far as possible along each branch before backtracking.

Best-First Search:

The best-first search algorithm is a heuristic search algorithm that explores a graph by expanding the node that is closest to the goal.

Bidirectional Search:

A bidirectional search algorithm searches from both the start and the goal simultaneously. This approach is especially useful when the path from the start to the goal is very long, as this can drastically reduce the search time, since the search needs only to go half as deep.

The algorithm is as follows:

Mark the start vertex as visited. For each vertex adjacent to the start vertex, mark the adjacent vertex as visited, and add it to a queue. Repeat the previous step with the goal vertex. While the queue is not empty: Dequeue a vertex and mark it as visited. If the vertex is equivalent to the goal vertex, then stop. For each vertex adjacent to the dequeued vertex, mark the adjacent vertex as visited, and add it to the queue.

If the algorithm is able to reach the goal vertex, it will also mark all of the vertices in the path from the start to the goal as visited.

Iterative Deepening Depth-First Search (IDDFS):

IDDFS is an extension to the 'depth-first search' algorithm in which we iteratively perform DFS upto a certain 'depth', and keep increasing this 'depth' after every iteration. This algorithm is guaranteed to find the goal state,if it exists, within 'O(bd)' time, where 'b' is the branching factor and 'd' is the depth of the shallowest goal state.

Informed (Heuristic)SearchStrategies:

Applying the 2-opt algorithm (or other algorithms) to the TSP problem, which is an NP-complete problem, is an example of a brute-force search.

The 2-opt algorithm is a heuristic algorithm, because it uses a heuristic function to evaluate the solution it generates.

The 2-opt algorithm is a greedy algorithm, because it makes the locally optimal choice at each step in the hope of finding a globally optimal solution.

Heuristic Evaluation Functions:

The following heuristic evaluation functions can be used to reduce the search space to a minimum, and then the best solution can be further improved by an exact search. The heuristic evaluation functions are defined as follows:

1) The heuristic evaluation function based on the number of jumps: The heuristic evaluation function is defined as,

2) The heuristic evaluation function based on the number of holes: The heuristic evaluation function is defined as,

3) The heuristic evaluation function based on the maximum number of blocks in a column: The heuristic evaluation function is defined as,

4) The heuristic evaluation function based on the sum of the absolute values of the differences between the height of adjacent columns: The heuristic evaluation function is defined as,

5) The heuristic evaluation function based on the sum of the absolute values of the differences between the height of adjacent rows: The heuristic evaluation function is defined as,

6) The heuristic evaluation function based on the sum of the absolute values of the differences between the height of adjacent columns and the height of adjacent rows: The heuristic evaluation function is defined as,

7) The heuristic evaluation function based on the square of the sum of the absolute

Pure Heuristic Search for Optimal Motion Planning on a Simple Grid world

This is a simple implementation of the A* algorithm to solve a basic grid world problem. The A* algorithm is a heuristic search algorithm that is used to find the shortest path from a starting node to a goal node. The algorithm uses a heuristic function to estimate the cost of the path from the starting node to the goal node. The heuristic function used in this implementation is the Manhattan Distance. The Manhattan Distance is the sum of the absolute values of the differences in the x-coordinates and the y-coordinates of the two nodes.

The grid world problem is defined as follows:

There is a grid with squares that are either empty or have an obstacle.

The start node is the green square and the goal node is the red square.

The agent can move up, down, left, or right.

The agent cannot move through obstacles.

The goal is to find the shortest path from the start node to the goal node.

The A* algorithm works as follows:

1. The algorithm starts at the start node and adds it to the open list.

2. The algorithm then expands the node with the lowest cost from

Local Search Algorithms:

The most general local search algorithm is the hill-climbing algorithm, which is defined as follows:

The algorithm starts at some arbitrary solution. While the solution is not optimal, it tries to find another solution that is better (higher-quality or lower-cost).

If it cannot find a better solution, it returns the current solution. The hill-climbing algorithm is very simple, but it is also very inefficient. It can get stuck in local optima, which are solutions that are not globally optimal but are better than all of the neighboring solutions.

The algorithm can be improved by adding a random restart: instead of starting at a single solution, the algorithm starts at multiple solutions and runs the hill-climbing algorithm independently on each of them. The best solution found by any of the runs is returned.

The algorithm can also be improved by using different types of neighborhood structures. A neighborhood is a set of solutions that can be reached from the current solution by making a small change.

Instead of considering all of the solutions in the neighborhood, the algorithm can be restricted to consider only the best solution in the neighborhood (the solution with the highest quality or the lowest cost).

Hill-Climbing Search:

Hill-climbing search is a local search algorithm that seeks to maximize a heuristic by incrementally moving in the direction of the steepest ascent until no further improvement can be made. The algorithm is an anytime algorithm, meaning that it can return a solution at any time, even if it is not the global optimum.

The algorithm begins at a random node and then chooses the successor node with the highest heuristic value. It then moves to that node and repeats the process.

If there are multiple nodes with the same heuristic value, the algorithm will choose one at random. If the algorithm reaches a point where there are no nodes with a higher heuristic value, it has reached a local optimum and will return the current solution.

The main advantage of hill-climbing search is that it is simple to implement and can often find good solutions quickly. The main disadvantage is that it can get stuck in local optima, meaning that it will not find the global optimum solution.

Local Beam Search:

A local beam search algorithm is a simple heuristic method used in a search algorithm to find an approximate solution to a problem. Local beam search is a state space search algorithm that uses a beam of search states to find a solution.

The algorithm expands the search state with the lowest cost and adds it to the beam. The beam is then expanded by one search state for each iteration of the algorithm. The algorithm terminates when a goal state is added to the beam or the beam is empty.

The algorithm is not guaranteed to find the optimal solution, but it is guaranteed to find a solution that is within a certain cost of the optimal solution. The cost of the solution is the sum of the costs of the search states in the beam

Simulated Annealing:

Simulated annealing is a heuristic search algorithm for solving optimization problems. It is often used when the search space is large or when the optimization problem is difficult to solve.

The algorithm works by starting with a random solution and then iteratively improving the solution by making small changes. The changes are made more randomly at first and then become more focused as the algorithm converges on a solution.

The hope is that the algorithm will find a global optimum, but it is not guaranteed to do so. The name and inspiration come from annealing in metallurgy, a technique involving heating and controlled cooling of a material to increase the size of its crystals and reduce their defects. Both are attributes that are important in the search for an optimal solution.

Travelling Salesman Problem:

The travelling salesman problem (TSP) is a problem in combinatorial optimisation, requiring the most efficient (least cost) route to be found between a number of cities. The problem arises in many practical applications, such as planning sales trips, routing vehicles and scheduling tasks.

The problem can be formally stated as follows: Given a list of n cities, with the distances between each pair of cities given, find the shortest possible route that visits each city exactly once and returns to the starting city.

The problem is known to be NP-hard, meaning that there is no known algorithm that can solve it in polynomial time (that is, with a running time that is a polynomial function of the size of the problem instance). Despite this, many heuristic and approximation algorithms have been developed that can find reasonable solutions to the problem in a reasonable amount of time.

The problem has been extensively studied and many variations and generalisations have been considered. These include the asymmetric TSP, in which the cost of travelling from city A to city B is not necessarily the same as the cost of travelling from city B to city A, and the stochastic TSP, in which the distances between cities are not known exactly.

CHAPTER SIX

Role of Fuzzy Logic Systems & NLP

What is Fuzzy Logic?

Fuzzy logic is a form of logic that deals with approximate, rather than exact, reasoning. Fuzzy logic is often used in artificial intelligence applications where precise data is not available.

Fuzzy logic is a type of logic that allows for partial truths, rather than the either/or truths of traditional Boolean logic. In Boolean logic, something is either true or false; in fuzzy logic, something can be partially true or partially false.

Why Fuzzy Logic?

Fuzzy logic is a form of mathematics that deals with approximate, rather than exact, values. It is often used in situations where traditional methods of mathematics would give imprecise or conflicting results.

Fuzzy logic is a type of logic that allows for partial truths, instead of the either/or truths of traditional boolean logic. This can be useful in situations where a definitive answer is not possible, or when there is ambiguity.

Fuzzy logic is a type of logic that allows for partial truths, instead of the either/or truths of classical logic. In classical logic, something is either true or false; in fuzzy logic, something can be partially true and partially false.

Fuzzy Logic SystemsArchitecture Of Fuzzy Logic Systems:

FUZZY LOGIC SYSTEMS

Fuzzy Logic Systems Fuzzy logic systems (FLSs) are a type of non-Boolean control system that has been employed in a variety of engineering applications in recent years.

Originally proposed by Lotfi Zadeh in 1965, fuzzy logic systems have the ability to utilize linguistic values instead of numerical values for input and output. This type of system is able to deal with imprecision, uncertainty, and approximate reasoning.

Fuzzy logic systems have been used in many diverse applications, including control of home appliances, automotive systems, and medical equipments.

Fuzzy logic systems are usually comprised of five main components:

• Fuzzifier: Converts crisp input values into fuzzy sets

. • Rule Base: Contains a set of IF-THEN rules that are used to map the inputs to outputs.

• Inference Engine: Processes the rules in the rule base and generates output values.

• Defuzzifier: Converts the output fuzzy set into a crisp value.

• Knowledge Base: Stores information about the system, such as membership functions and rule base

Membership Functions

The membership function is a mathematical function that maps an element of a given input domain to a real number in the interval [0,1]. The function determines how much an arbitrary element of the domain belongs to the given set.

This is the membership function of a fuzzy set A.

Types of membership functions:

There are three main types of membership functions:

Triangular: this is the simplest type. It is defined by three points (a, 0), (m, 1), (b, 0). This type is usually used for linguistic variables that can be defined with words like "very low", "medium" and "very high".

This is the simplest type. It is defined by three points (a, 0), (m, 1), (b, 0). This type is usually used for linguistic variables that can be defined with words like "very low", "medium" and "very high".

Trapezoidal: this type is defined by four points (a, 0), (m1, 0), (m2, 1), (b, 0). It is used for linguistic variables that can be defined with words like "very low", "low", "high" and "very.

Example of a Fuzzy Logic System:

Fuzzy logic systems are often used in control systems, where they can help a machine make decisions based on incomplete or imprecise data. For example, a washing machine might use a fuzzy logic system to determine how much water to use based on the size of the load and the dirtiness of the clothes.

Fuzzy logic systems are often used in industrial applications because they can be designed to mimic the decision-making process of a human operator.

For example, a fuzzy logic system could be used to control the speed of a conveyor belt in a manufacturing plant. The system would take into account factors such as the weight of the objects on the belt and the desired speed of the belt. The system would then use fuzzy logic to determine the optimal speed for the belt.

A Fuzzy Logic System (FLS) is a system that uses fuzzy logic to make decisions. Fuzzy logic is a type of logic that allows for approximate reasoning. This means that it can deal with imprecise or incomplete information.

FLSs are used in a variety of fields, including control systems, artificial intelligence, and decision support systems. They have been used in a wide range of applications, such as automotive systems, medical diagnosis, and stock market analysis.

FLSs typically have three components:

1. A fuzzifier, which converts input data into a fuzzy set.

2. A rule base, which contains a set of rules that define the relationships between inputs and outputs.

3. A defuzzifier, which converts the output of the rule base into a crisp value.

Application Areas of Fuzzy Logic:

Fuzzy logic has a very large range of applications. Some of the main areas in which fuzzy logic can be used are as follows:

1. Image Processing

2. Pattern Recognition

3. Data Mining

4. Control Systems

5. Robotics

6. Natural Language Processing

7. Artificial Intelligence

8. Big Data Analytics

9. Predictive Analytics

Image Processing: Fuzzy logic can be used in image processing in order to make better decisions about the image. It can also help to process the image faster.

Pattern Recognition:

Fuzzy logic can be used in pattern recognition in order to make better decisions about the pattern. It can also help to process the pattern faster.

Data Mining:

Fuzzy logic can be used in data mining in order to make better decisions about the data. It can also help to process the data faster.

Control Systems:

Fuzzy logic can be used in control systems in order to make better decisions about the system. It can also help to process the system faster.

Robotics:

Fuzzy logic can be used in robotics in order to make better decisions about the robot.

Advantages of FLSs:

1. FLSs can be used to create customized lighting solutions for specific needs.

2. FLSs are more energy efficient than traditional light sources, such as incandescent bulbs.

3. FLSs do not produce as much heat as traditional light sources, making them safer to use in many applications.

4. FLSs can last for many years, saving money on replacement costs.

5. FLSs are available in a variety of colors and intensities, allowing for greater flexibility in lighting design.

Disadvantages of FLSs:

There are several disadvantages of FLSs to consider:

1. They are expensive.

2. They are not always accurate.

3. They can be difficult to use.

4. They can be time-consuming.

One serious disadvantage of FLSs is that they may be postulated to exist on the basis of certain observations, but they may never be observed directly.

Another disadvantage is that FLSs are often proposed to explain phenomena that are poorly understood, and this can lead to a lot of research that is ultimately fruitless.

Natural Language Processing

Natural language processing (NLP) is a field of computer science, artificial intelligence, and linguistics concerned with the interactions between computers and human (natural) languages.

As such, NLP is related to the area of human-computer interaction. Many challenges in NLP involve teaching computers to effectively process, understand, and generate human language content.

Components of NLP:

There are three main components to NLP:

1. The linguistic component: This involves understanding the structure of language and how it can be used to create meaning.

2. The cognitive component: This involves understanding how the mind works and how it processes information.

3. The behavioral component: This involves understanding how behavior is created and how it can be changed.

Difficulties in NLU:

There are a few major issues in NLU:

1. Language ambiguity: There are many words in English (and other languages) that have multiple meanings, which can make it difficult for machines to understand which meaning is intended in a given context. For example, the word "bass" can refer to a type of fish, a musical instrument, or a low frequency sound.

2. Idioms and slang: Idioms and slang are often used in everyday speech and can be difficult for machines to understand. For example, the phrase "I'm pulling your leg" is an idiom that means "I'm joking with you."

3. Ambiguous pronouns: Pronouns such as "it" or "they" can be ambiguous and difficult for machines to interpret. For example, the sentence "John is taller than he" is difficult for a machine to parse because it is unclear who the pronoun "he" is referring to.

4. World knowledge: In order to understand the meaning of a sentence, a machine needs to have some knowledge of the world. For example, the sentence "The sun is a star" is only true if the machine knows that the sun is a star.

NLP Terminology:

Machine Learning:

A method of teaching computers to learn from data, without being explicitly programmed.

Natural Language Processing (NLP):

A subfield of computer science, artificial intelligence, and linguistics concerned with the interactions between computers and human (natural) languages.

Text classification:

The process of assigning tags or categories to text according to its content. For example, an email spam filter examines new emails and classify them according to whether they are spam or not.

Sentiment analysis:

The use of natural language processing, text analysis, computational linguistics, and biometrics to systematically identify, extract, quantify, and study affective states and subjective information.

Sentiment analysis is widely applied to voice of the customer materials such as reviews and survey responses, online and social media, and healthcare materials for applications that range from marketing to customer service to clinical medicine.

Steps in NLP:
1. Pre-processing
2. Tokenization
3. Tagging
4. Chunking
5. Parsing
6. Semantic Analysis
7. Discourse
8. Pragmatic Analysis
9. Semantics
10. Pragmatics

Implementation Aspects of Syntactic Analysis:

The purpose of the syntactic analysis phase is to find the syntactic structure of a sentence. It is a question of constructing a tree whose leaves are the words of the sentence, and whose branches are the syntactic relations between these words.

The notion of syntactic structure expressed in the form of a tree is a very abstract one. It is expressed in terms of a set of relations between the words of the sentence. There are different approaches to syntactic analysis, which define the concepts of syntactic relations in different ways.

The most popular approach to syntactic analysis is the approach known as transformational grammar. This approach was developed by Noam Chomsky.

Transformational grammar is based on the idea that there are two levels of syntactic structure: the level of deep structure, and the level of surface structure. The level of deep structure is the level of syntactic structure that corresponds to the meaning of the sentence.

The level of surface structure is the level of syntactic structure that corresponds to the form of the sentence. The transformational grammar approach to syntactic analysis is based on the idea that there are two types of syntactic relations: theta relations and case relations. Theta relations are relations between a verb and its arguments.

CHAPTER SEVEN

AI-Expert Systems

Expert systems are computer programs that simulate the decision-making ability of a human expert. They are designed to solve complex problems by reasoning through a set of rules, just as a human expert would.

Expert systems are built using a knowledge base, which contains all of the information that the expert system needs to know in order to make decisions.

This knowledge is typically encoded in the form of rules. For example, a rule might state that if a patient has a fever and a rash, then they likely have chickenpox.

What are Expert Systems?

Expert systems are computer programs that simulate the decision-making ability of human experts. They are designed to solve complex problems by reasoning through bodies of knowledge, using a process that mimics human thinking.

Capabilities of Expert Systems:

Expert systems have proven to be very useful in a number of different domains. They have been used in medicine for diagnosis, in business for financial analysis and in manufacturing for quality control.

Expert systems are able to provide explanations for their decisions, which is a major advantage over traditional computer systems.

They can also be used to generate new knowledge by reasoning from a set of facts. Expert systems are not perfect, however, and there are some limitations to their capabilities.

They can be expensive to develop and maintain, and they require a high level of expertise to use effectively. Additionally, expert systems can be biased by the knowledge and experience of the developers.

Components of Expert Systems:

An expert system consists of four main components.

1. Knowledge base

2. Inference engine

3. User interface

4. Explanation facility

1.Knowledge Base:

The knowledge base stores the rules, and the data that are required for the expert system to function. It is the heart of the expert system and contains the entire expert knowledge in the form of rules.

2.Inference Engine:

The inference engine is used to execute the rules stored in the knowledge base. It is used to make a decision based on the rules and data stored in the knowledge base.

3. User Interface:

This is the part of the expert system through which the user interacts with the system. It is used to input data and receive results from the system.

4. Explanation Facility:

The explanation facility is used to explain the reasoning behind the decision made by the expert system. It is used to provide justification for the decision made by the system.

Knowledge Base (KB):

A knowledge base (KB) is a repository of information designed to capture, organize, and share knowledge. A KB can take many forms, including a database, a document, or a set of rules or procedures.

A knowledge base can be used to store information about a particular subject, such as a company or product. A KB can also be used to store information about a specific process or procedure. In either case, a knowledge base can be a valuable tool for sharing information and knowledge within an organization.

A knowledge base can be created manually or automatically. Manual creation typically involves the use of a text editor, such as Microsoft Word, to create a document. Automatic creation can be accomplished using a variety of software applications, such as a database application or a word processing application.

A knowledge base can be used for a variety of purposes, such as providing customer support, maintaining product documentation, or sharing best practices within an organization.

What is Knowledge in AI?

In AI, knowledge is defined as a collection of facts and information that has been organized in a way that is easy for computers to understand and use.

Components of Knowledge Base:

A knowledge base typically contains three different types of components:

data store:

This is where all of the knowledge base's data is stored. This data can be in the form of text, images, videos, or anything else that can be stored digitally.

knowledge base software:

This is the software that is used to manage and maintain the knowledge base. This software typically includes features such as search, categorization, and access control.

user interface:

This is how users interact with the knowledge base. This can be a web-based interface, a desktop application, or a mobile app.

Inference Engine:

The Inference Engine is composed of a set of libraries that allow you to load, process, and perform inference on your models. The Inference Engine also supports traditional CNN architectures and other DNN types.

Model Optimizer:

The Model Optimizer is a cross-platform command-line tool that takes a trained model and converts it to an optimized intermediate representation (IR). The Model Optimizer is a key component of the overall Intel® one API Model Optimization Toolkit.

The Intel® one API Model Optimization Toolkit is a free and open-source toolkit for developing and deploying deep learning and computer vision applications using the Intel® Distribution of OpenVINO™ Toolkit.

Forward Chaining:

In forward chaining the system starts from the known facts and moves forward in search of new facts. This is the way humans learn. When a person learns something new, it is integrated with the information already stored in his mind and new conclusions are drawn.

Backward Chaining:

In backward chaining the system starts from the desired goal and moves backward to find the facts that lead to it. This is the way a child learns. When a child learns something new, he starts from the desired goal and moves backward to find the facts that lead to it.

Forward Chaining:

When you have a chain of rules where the conclusion of one rule becomes the premise of the next rule, you have forward chaining. This can help you remember rules and logical arguments.

Example:

You have a list of things you need to do in order to go on vacation.

1. Buy a ticket

2. Pack a suitcase

3. Get a passport

You can remember these steps by chaining them together: "I need to buy a ticket, pack a suitcase, and get a passport before I can go on vacation."

Backward Chaining:

Backward chaining is when you work from the conclusion to the premises. This can be helpful when you are trying to solve a problem and you know the solution, but you need to figure out the steps to get there.

Example:

You want to make a cake. You know that you need flour, sugar, eggs, and butter. But you don't have any eggs. You can use backward chaining to figure out what you need to do: "I need eggs to make a cake. I need to go to the store to get eggs."

User Interface:

The user interface of the Avira antivirus is extremely easy to navigate. It does not feature any unnecessary things and everything you need can be found within a few clicks. For instance, the main interface features a large green scan button that can be used to start a quick scan on your computer. The main interface also features a large icon that shows you the overall protection level of your computer.

The settings menu of the Avira antivirus is very user-friendly as well. It is divided into sections and each section is clearly labeled. You will have no problem finding the setting you want to change.

Features:

The Avira antivirus comes with all the features you need to protect your computer from malware and viruses. It has a real-time protection module that blocks malicious files and websites. It also features a heuristic engine that can detect unknown viruses. The Avira antivirus also features a rootkit removal tool that can remove rootkits from your computer.

The Avira antivirus also comes with a Firewall module that can block incoming and outgoing network connections. It also has an AntiSpam module that can block unwanted emails. The Avira antivirus also features a Browser Protection module that can block malicious websites.

Requirements of Efficient ES User Interface:

1. The ES user interface should be intuitive and easy to use.

2. The ES user interface should be designed for both novice and expert users.

3. The ES user interface should be able to handle large amounts of data.

4. The ES user interface should be able to handle multiple user requests.

5. The ES user interface should be able to provide customized reports.

Expert Systems Limitations:

1. The system should be capable of handling large volumes of data.

2. The system should be capable of handling data with missing or incomplete values.

3. The system should be capable of dealing with imprecise data.

4. The system should be capable of managing many different types of constraints.

5. The system should be capable of handling data that are constantly changing.

Applications of Expert System:

Expert systems are used in various fields, including:

* Medicine: expert systems are used to diagnose diseases, recommend treatments, and interpret test results.

* Law: expert systems are used to offer legal advice and predict the outcomes of court cases.

* Business: expert systems are used in marketing, finance, and project management.

* Education: expert systems are used to tutor students and offer guidance on careers.

* Science: expert systems are used to interpret data from experiments and make predictions.

Expert System Technology (EST):

This technology is used to create expert systems. A knowledge engineer writes a program that captures the knowledge of a human expert in a specific field. This program typically includes a rule base and a reasoning system.

This refers to the technology that is used for developing the expert system. It includes knowledge acquisition, knowledge representation, reasoning, and explanation.

Forward chaining:

This is a type of reasoning in which the system moves from the current state to the goal state, by deriving new information.

Heuristic:

This is a method or rule of thumb that is used in problem-solving, when the problem cannot be solved by using a simple method. It is a type of rule-based reasoning, which is also known as knowledge-based reasoning.

Inference engine:

This is a type of expert system that uses a knowledge base and reasoning to solve problems. It uses a set of rules to determine how to solve a problem.

Inference rule:

This is a rule that is used by an inference engine to solve a problem.

Knowledge base:

This is the part of an expert system that contains the knowledge that is used by the system to solve problems.

Knowledge engineering:

This is the process of developing an expert system. It includes knowledge acquisition, knowledge representation, reasoning, and explanation.

Knowledge representation:

This is the process of representing knowledge in a format that can be used by an expert system.

Development of Expert Systems:

- Expert Systems are computer based systems that are designed to make decisions and provide recommendations or advice, as well as to explain their rationale, as if they were human experts.

-An expert system is a computer program that uses artificial intelligence (AI) techniques to solve complex problems or perform complex tasks.

-Expert systems are designed to mimic the decision-making ability of a human expert.

-The first expert system was developed in the early 1970s by a research team at Stanford University. -Expert systems became commercially available in the early 1980s.

-Expert systems are used in a variety of fields, including medicine, finance, manufacturing, and engineering.

Benefits of Expert Systems:

Expert systems have many benefits over conventional systems. They can provide better decision making, improve efficiency and productivity, and reduce costs.

Improved Decision Making:

Expert systems can provide better decision making by providing accurate and up-to-date information. They can also help decision makers to make better decisions by providing expert advice.

Improved Efficiency and Productivity:

Expert systems can help to improve efficiency and productivity by automating tasks. They can also help to reduce errors and improve quality control.

Reduced Costs:

Expert systems can help to reduce costs by automating tasks and reducing the need for human resources. They can also help to improve quality control and reduce the time required to complete tasks.

CHAPTER EIGHT

AI-Robotics & Neural Networks

Robotics is a branch of engineering that deals with the design and construction of robots. Robotics engineering includes the study of robotic systems and their interactions with the environment, as well as the design and implementation of robotic devices.

Robotics engineers may also be involved in the development of new applications for robotics technology. Robotics is a rapidly growing field, with new applications being found all the time. Currently, robots are used in a variety of industries including manufacturing, healthcare, agriculture, and even the military. As the capabilities of robots continue to expand, so too will the number of industries in which they are used.

What are Robots?

A robot is a machine that is able to carry out a series of complex tasks automatically. robots are increasingly becoming part of our everyday lives, carrying out tasks that are dangerous, difficult or simply boring.

What is Robotics?

Robotics is the branch of technology that deals with the design and operation of robots. Robots are machines that can be programmed to carry out a variety of tasks, including moving objects, sensing and processing information, and performing human-like activities.

Aspects of Robotics and Automation:

The term robotics refers to the technology and engineering discipline that designs, develops, and builds robots. Robotics is a branch of engineering that deals with the design, construction, operation, and applications of robots. Robotics is related to the fields of electronics, mechatronics, and computer science.

Robots are widely used in manufacturing, assembly, and packaging, as well as in military, space, and consumer applications. Robotics is also used in medicine, surgery, and prosthetics.

Robots are usually designed to perform a specific task or set of tasks. They may be programmed to carry out these tasks autonomously, or they may be controlled by a human operator.

Robots can be classified into two main types: industrial robots and service robots. Industrial robots are used in manufacturing and assembly tasks, while service robots are used in tasks such as healthcare, cleaning, and personal assistance.

Industrial robots are classified into three main types: Cartesian robots, cylindrical robots, and articulated robots. Cartesian robots are the most common type of industrial robot, and they are used in tasks such as pick-and-place, welding, and material handling. Cylindrical robots are used in tasks such as packaging.

Robot locomotion:

Robot Locomotion refers to the various ways in which robots can move from place to place. The most common type of locomotion for robots is wheeled locomotion, in which the robot moves on wheels. Other types of locomotion include legged locomotion, in which the robot moves on legs, and flying locomotion, in which the robot moves through the air using wings or rotors.

Robot locomotion is the ability of a robot to move itself from one place to another. Locomotion can be broadly classified into two types: legged and wheeled.

Legged robots are more complex and less efficient than wheeled robots, but they can move over rough terrain and are more stable.

The choice of locomotion type depends on the application. For example, legged robots are better suited for search and rescue missions, while wheeled robots are better suited for industrial applications.

There are many different ways to achieve robot locomotion. The most common are wheels, treads, legs, and flippers.

Wheels are the simplest and most common form of locomotion. They are used on many types of robots, from vacuum cleaners to industrial robots.

Treads are similar to wheels, but they have a continuous loop of material that provides traction. Treads are used on some legged robots, such as the Mars rover, and on some wheeled robots.

Legged Locomotion:

Locomotion using a pair of legs is the most common form of locomotion in animals, found in arthropods (including insects, crabs, lobsters, and millipedes), tetrapods (including amphibians, reptiles, birds and mammals) and a number of other animals. Bipedalism is a form of locomotion where an organism moves by means of its two rear limbs, or legs.

There are three main types of bipedal locomotion. In human beings, human walking is the most common form of bipedal locomotion. The second most common form is running. The third is hopping, which is a series of short jumps.

There are many advantages to bipedal locomotion. Bipedal animals can cover more ground than quadruped animals. Bipedal animals can also travel over rougher terrain than quadrupedal animals. Bipedal animals can also carry more weight than quadruped animals.

The disadvantage of bipedal locomotion is that it is more energy intensive than quadrupedal locomotion. Bipedal animals also have a higher center of gravity, which makes them more likely to fall over.

Bipedal animals include: humans, kang

Components of a Robot:

The components of a robot must be designed to work together to achieve the robot's desired functionality. The most important components of a robot are its sensors, actuators, and control system.

Sensors:

Sensors are devices that detect and measure physical quantities such as light, sound, temperature, pressure, or motion. They convert these physical quantities into electrical signals that can be processed by the robot's control system. Sensors are essential for robots because they allow the robot to gather information about its surroundings.

Actuators:

Actuators are devices that produce physical movement or force. They convert electrical signals from the robot's control system into mechanical energy. Actuators are essential for robots because they allow the robot to interact with its surroundings.

Control System:

The control system is the heart of the robot. It is responsible for processing information from the robot's sensors, making decisions, and activating the robot's actuators. The control system can be either digital or analog. Digital control systems are made up of electronic components such as microprocessors, while analog control systems are made up of mechanical components such as gears and levers.

Computer vision:

Computer vision is a field of computer science that deals with how computers can be made to gain high-level understanding from digital images or videos.

CV is defined as a branch of computer science that deals with providing computers with an ability to see and process images in the same way that humans do. It involves the development of algorithms that can interpret an image and understand what is happening in that image.

Computer vision is a field of computer science that deals with how computers can be made to gain high-level understanding from digital images or videos.

Computer vision is the process of extracting meaning from images. It is a field of computer science that deals with the theory and application of artificial intelligence, machine learning, and computer vision.

Computer vision is a subfield of computer science that deals with the extraction, analysis, and understanding of useful information from digital images. It is closely related to fields such as image processing, pattern recognition, and machine vision.

Hardware of Computer Vision System:

The hardware of a computer vision system can be divided into two main categories:

- Input
- Output

Input devices are used to capture images from the real world. The most common input devices are digital cameras, which use an array of light-sensitive pixels to capture an image. Other input devices include infrared cameras, X-ray cameras, and scanning devices such as line scanners and barcode scanners.

Output devices are used to display the images captured by the input devices. The most common output devices are monitors, which display the images in a format that can be viewed by the human eye. Other output devices include printers, which can print out the images, and storage devices, which can save the images for later use.

Tasks of Computer Vision:

The tasks of computer vision can be divided into two groups:

1. **Geometric tasks:**

These tasks are concerned with the interpretation of image data that are acquired from a sensor. They include tasks such as image registration, object detection, object recognition, and 3D reconstruction.

2. Photometric tasks:

These tasks are concerned with the process of acquiring, analyzing, and understanding digital images. They include tasks such as image enhancement, image restoration, and image segmentation.

Application Domains of Computer Vision:

There are many application domains of computer vision, but the main application domain that we focus on in this book is image analysis. Image analysis is a broad term that covers many topics, including image acquisition, image processing, image understanding, and image visualization. Image analysis has a wide range of applications, including medical images, video, and multimedia.

Image Acquisition:

Image acquisition is the process of acquiring digital images from a physical source. The source can be a digital camera, a scanner, or a microscope. The digital images can be in the form of photos, videos, or 3D images.

Image Processing:

Image processing is the process of manipulating digital images to improve their quality or to extract useful information from them. The process can involve image enhancement, image restoration, and image analysis.

Image Enhancement:

Image enhancement is the process of improving the quality of digital images. The process can involve image sharpening, noise reduction, and color correction.

Image Restoration:

Image restoration is the process of repairing digital images that are damaged or corrupted. The process can involve image inpainting, image denoising, and image super-resolution.

Image Analysis:

Image analysis is the process of extracting useful information from digital.

Applications of Robotics:

There are many potential applications for robotics technology, including:

- Aerospace and defense
- Agriculture
- Automotive
- Construction
- Customer service
- Disaster response
- Domestic tasks
- Drug discovery and development
- Education
- Environmental monitoring
- Healthcare
- Hospitality
- Manufacturing
- Mining
- Personal assistance
- Security
- Space exploration
- Telecommunications
- Urban planning
- Warehousing and logistics
- **Robotics technology** is also increasingly being used in research and development. For example, robots are being used to explore extreme environments such as the bottom of the ocean or the surface of other planets.

. Neural Networks

The term neural network was originally used to refer to a network or circuit of biological neurons. The modern usage of the term often refers to artificial neural networks, which are composed of artificial neurons or nodes.

Neural networks are often used for image recognition, pattern recognition, and identification of trends or anomalies. Neural networks can be trained to perform a variety of tasks, including classification, prediction, and optimization.

What are Artificial Neural Networks (ANNs)?

ANNs are a type of machine learning algorithm that are used to model complex patterns in data. ANNs are similar to the human brain in that they are composed of a series of interconnected nodes, or neurons, that can learn to recognize patterns of input data.

Basic Structure of ANNs:

The basic structure of a neural network consists of a set of units (neurons) connected by directed weighted links.

This structure is capable of storing and retrieving information by means of pattern association.

Each neuron is connected to other neurons by weighted links.

The weight of a link indicates the strength of the connection between the two neurons.

The input to a neuron is the weighted sum of all the inputs from the neurons connected to it.

A neuron produces an output by applying a non-linear function to the input. Learning in Neural Networks Learning in neural networks can be either supervised or unsupervised.

In supervised learning, the training data contains both the input patterns and the desired output patterns.

The neural network is trained to produce the desired output for a given input pattern. In unsupervised learning, the training data contains only the input patterns.

The neural network is trained to recognize patterns in the data.

Types of Artificial Neural Networks:

There are three primary types of artificial neural networks:

Feed forward neural networks are the simplest type of neural network and are used to map input data to output data without any feedback loops.

Recurrent neural networks have feedback loops, allowing them to model temporal data.

Convolution neural networks are specialized for processing data that has a spatial structure, such as images.

Feed Forward ANN:

Feed Forward ANNs are just simple neural networks in which the neurons are connected in the feed-forward direction.

Back propagation is a method for training neural networks. It uses an algorithm to figure out how to adjust the weights of the connections (edges) between neurons so that the network can learn to produce the correct output for a given input.

Artificial neural networks are a type of machine learning algorithm that is used to model complex patterns in data. Neural networks are similar to other machine learning algorithms, but they are composed of a large number of interconnected processing nodes, or neurons, that can learn to recognize patterns of input data.

- **Working of ANNs:**

Artificial Neural Networks work in a similar way to the natural neural networks present in our brain. The brain consists of a large number of interconnected neurons. The information from a neuron is passed through the dendrites to the next neuron. This process continues until the information reaches its desired destination.

ANNs consist of interconnected layers called neurons. The input layer contains neurons that receive the input data. The hidden layer contains neurons that process the data. The output layer contains neurons that return the results. Each neuron in the hidden layer is connected to each neuron in the input layer and output layer.

ANNs are trained using a method called back propagation. The error is calculated between the actual and predicted values. This error is back propagated through the hidden layer to the input layer. The weights of the hidden layer are updated to minimize the error. This process is repeated until the error is minimized.

Advantages of Artificial Neural Networks:
ANNs can handle non-linear problems.
ANNs can handle complex problems.
ANNs can learn from data. ANNs can generalize from data.
ANNs can be trained to perform tasks.
Machine Learning in ANNs :
Machine learning is a process of teaching computers to learn from data. This is done by providing the computer with a set of training data, which is a set of data that includes both the input data and the desired output. The computer then uses this training data to learn how to map the input data to the desired output.

ANNs are particularly well suited for machine learning tasks because they are able to learn complex relationships between the input and output data.

Back Propagation Algorithm for Neural Network:

The back propagation algorithm is a neural network training algorithm. It is a supervised learning algorithm. The algorithm propagates the error gradient back through the neural network to update the weights of the network.

The back propagation algorithm is a gradient descent algorithm. The error gradient is calculated using the back propagation algorithm.

The back propagation algorithm is an efficient algorithm for training neural networks. The back propagation algorithm has been found to be very effective in training neural networks. The back propagation algorithm is used in many neural network applications.

Bayesian Networks (BN):

Bayesian networks are a graphical model that represents a set of variables and their conditional dependencies.

A Bayesian network is composed of:

Nodes: Each node represents a variable.

Edges: Edges represent the dependencies between the variables.

Conditional Probability Tables (CPTs): Each node has a CPT that specifies the probability of each value of the variable, given the values of its parents.

Building a Bayesian Network:

A Bayesian network is a graphical model that encodes probabilistic relationships among variables of interest. Bayesian networks are ideally suited to representing situations where there is uncertainty, and they can be used to make predictions about the likelihood of different events occurring.

To build a Bayesian network, you will need to specify the variables that you want to include in the model and the relationships between them. You will also need to specify the prior probabilities for each of the variables. These probabilities can be estimated from data, or they can be set based on expert knowledge.

Once the network is specified, you can use it to make predictions about new data. For example, if you have a Bayesian network that represents the relationships between medical symptoms and diseases, you can use it to predict the likelihood of a patient having a particular disease based on their symptoms.

BNs can be used for a number of tasks, including:

Classification: Given a set of observations, a BN can be used to classify the observations into different classes.

Prediction: A BN can be used to predict the value of a variable, given the values of other variables.

Diagnosis: A BN can be used to diagnose a problem, by reasoning about the causes of the problem.

Decision Making: A BN can be used to make decisions, by reasoning about the possible consequences of different actions.

AI Issues:

How can I restock AI-controlled shops?

You can restock them by selling them items. Only items that are available for purchase at the AI-controlled shops will be considered for restocking.

How can I get the AI to stop attacking me?

You can get them to stop attacking you by attacking them. After they get low on health they will stop attacking you.

How can I get the AI to start attacking me?

You can get them to start attacking you by attacking them. After they get low on health they will stop attacking you.

Threat to Privacy:

The biggest threat to Data privacy is the loss of data confidentiality. Data privacy is the unauthorized use or disclosure of personal information. The most common type of data privacy breach is identity theft. Identity theft occurs when someone uses your personal information, without your permission, to commit fraud or other crimes.

Threat to Human Dignity:

The trend toward surveillance and suppression of dissent that is currently being witnessed in many countries is a grave threat to the dignity of the person, because it threatens the very core of human freedom and self-determination.

As the International Covenant on Civil and Political Rights states, "the inherent dignity of the human person is the foundation of freedom, justice, and peace in the world." This dignity is the dignity of the person as a free being, who is capable of making choices and decisions about what to do with his or her life.

When a government engages in surveillance and suppression of dissent, it is violating the dignity of the individuals it is targeting. It is treating them as if they are not free beings, but rather as objects to be controlled and manipulated. This is a grave injustice that must be opposed.

Threat to Safety:

The exposure to deadly viruses, bacteria and other harmful agents will put everybody at risk. If a single person gets infected, it is highly likely that he or she will infect all others.

The other members of the household will also be at high risk. The same goes for members of the community. The spread of the deadly virus or bacteria will be rapid and will put a lot of people at risk.

Economic Impact:

The outbreak of deadly viruses and bacteria can have a detrimental effect on the economy. This is because the production of goods and services will be disrupted.

The outbreak of deadly viruses and bacteria can also lead to the closure of businesses. This is because the customers will be afraid to patronize the businesses. The closure of businesses will lead to job losses.

The outbreak of deadly viruses and bacteria can also lead to the rise in the prices of goods and services. This is because the businesses will be forced to increase their prices in order to cover the cost of production.

CHAPTER NINE

AI Terminology

The term artificial intelligence was coined by John McCarthy, who defined it as "the science and engineering of making intelligent machines." McCarthy is often credited as the father of AI.

The term intelligent agent was coined by Marvin Minsky, who defined it as "a system that perceives its environment and takes actions that maximize its chances of success."

Agent:

An agent is an entity that operates on an environment to reach some goal.

Autonomous Robot:

An autonomous robot is a robot that is capable of carrying out tasks without human intervention.

Backward Chaining:

In Artificial Intelligence, backward chaining is a reasoning method used to derive conclusions from a set of given facts. It is also sometimes called backward reasoning or retrograde analysis.

The backward chaining algorithm works by first identifying the goal, and then working backwards to identify the steps that must be taken in order to achieve the goal. Once the steps have been identified, the algorithm then works forwards to identify any subgoals that need to be achieved in order to complete the overall goal.

Blackboard:

A blackboard is a knowledge representation technique used in artificial intelligence (AI) that enables a system to store and retrieve knowledge in a flexible manner. The blackboard model was introduced by AI researchers in the late 1960s and has been used in a variety of AI applications since then.